Renaissance Painting Techniques That Every Painter Should Know

Clintond J. Hill

Introduction

This is a comprehensive guide that delves into the principles and practices of art composition during the Renaissance period. This guide explores the concepts and methods employed by Renaissance painters to create visually captivating and harmonious works of art.

The first section of the guide focuses on the concept of composition, explaining what it is, why it matters, and how it is executed in art. The emphasis is on the significance of composition in creating compelling visual narratives and communicating emotions through the arrangement of elements on the canvas.

The guide then delves into the theory behind Renaissance painting, presenting the rules of Renaissance composition. These rules encompass various techniques and approaches, including the Rule of Thirds, groupings in threes, geometric shapes, simple 'musical' proportions, harmonic grids, use of perspective, and the utilization of diagonals in the composition.

As the guide progresses, it explores specific concepts like the Golden Mean, symmetry and asymmetry, contrapposto (a pose conveying natural movement and balance), and the role of mass, colors, and tones in the composition.

The Process of Composition and Painting in the Renaissance section takes readers through the step-by-step journey of creating a Renaissance painting. From compositional sketches and detailed study drawings to the final painting, it highlights the thorough planning and preparation involved in producing masterpieces.

Concerning Proportion is another crucial topic discussed in the guide, particularly the Canon of Human Proportions and various proportions related to the head, face, and hands. Arranging figures in groups, symbolism, and the size of figures in relation to the composition are also covered in detail.

The guide goes on to explore different oil painting techniques used during the Renaissance, including the materials employed and the various styles used by painters from different regions.

A section on Leonardo da Vinci focuses on his painting techniques and also includes a comparison of portraits believed to represent him.

To provide a more comprehensive understanding, the guide concludes with an appendix on perspective, encompassing overlapping objects, atmospheric perspective, perspective of disappearance, vertical perspective, and perspective of size (linear perspective).

This comprehensive guide serves as a valuable resource for artists, art enthusiasts, and history lovers, offering insights into the artistic techniques and thought processes that contributed to the timeless beauty of Renaissance art.

Contents

On Composition

What is Composition?

A good composition has **unity**, **variety** and **balance**. It **unifies** the painting so that one item leads gently to another without jarring the observer. The composition must also have enough **variety** that it maintains the interest of the viewer. **Balance** in the composition is necessary as people find unbalanced paintings disturbing. Balance does not depend on symmetry, but on the perceived distribution and mass of shapes, tones and colours. Composition is the process of designing and putting together the elements that make up a painting (or sculpture) so as to satisfactorily accomplish these aims.

Why Composition?

A good painting has many attributes. It conveys an idea, feeling or emotion and may tell a story to entertain or educate. A good composition will draw the eye of the viewer to the main subject of the painting and will then lead the eye over all the regions of the canvas. The painting must be skilfully composed so as to do this in an interesting way. It does this by the use of Tone, Contrast, Line, Shape and Colour. The reason we compose our paintings is to enable the painting to convey the idea or emotion that we wish to communicate with the viewer.

How to do Composition?

Composition is an art not a science. It is a process of trial and error, and judgement. It consists of a series of incremental improvements of a design based on the judgement of the painter.

Many sketches may be made to come up with a design and test it, to determine the best composition. Usually these sketches are small, no bigger than 100mm x 150mm (known as 'thumbnails' or 'compositional sketches'). These are produced to determine the best

1

locations for the large shapes and tonal areas. A suggested process is to produce three or four thumbnail sketches of the subject, all different, and then stand back and judge which one or two are the most pleasing. Then, take these better thumbnails and try to improve on them and refine the composition by making further thumbnail sketches, each one adjusted slightly differently. You may try applying different compositional rules when developing these compositions to see if these improve your picture. These refined sketches are judged and the best selected. This process should be regarded as an intellectual game, to be enjoyed for its own sake.

To help train your artistic judgement it is best to view and study many works of art by established great painters, the old masters, and try to understand the elements of each composition and how they relate to the compositional rules which are given in this book. It is also necessary to try to understand where the compositional rules have been deviated from, and why.

Here are some examples of thumbnail sketches from my notebook. They are not necessarily in the Renaissance style, but they give an indication of the types of preliminary sketches you might produce:

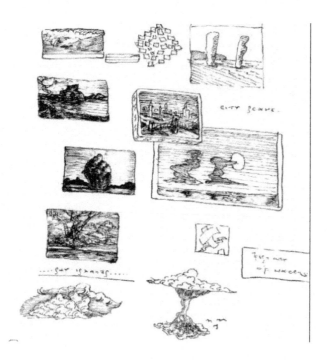

CITY SCENE.

....SKY ISLANDS....

Notes on Renaissance Painting Theory

According to Giorgio Vasari, the Florentine Renaissance artist and art critic (and writer of the celebrated 'Lives of the Artists') who lived from 1511 AD to 1574 AD, the Italian Renaissance painting style included the following aspects:

1. Natura (Nature) - The imitation of nature. However, strict reproduction or copying falls short of perfection, as the physical world is considered to be imperfect. The subject must be improved on, in line with the Platonic ideal (the perfect conception) in the mind of the painter. The work is based on a knowledge of natural forms and from works of art from the past. Nature is used as a starting point and forms a constant reference. The artist must use imitation and judgement.

2. Grazia (Grace) – The work of art must be endowed with grace. Grace is an important feature requiring judgement of the eye. It is a softness, with smooth transitions, and an appropriateness.

3. Designo (Design) - Design, draughtsmanship and drawing. Drawing was the foundation of Renaissance art. Painting was the filling in of outlines. The object drawn must show what the artist sees and also the perfect form existing in the artist's mind.

4. Decoro (Decorum) - Decorum or Appropriateness of gestures, expression and clothes. The setting, gestures, expressions, and clothes of figures in a painting should reflect the character of the subject. Decorum is also considering the suitability of the work to its surroundings, such as whether it is in a church or a domestic dwelling.

5. Iudizio (Judgement) - Painter's judgement is a faculty of the eye which comes into play after the artist has observed the rules of imitation (natura), measurement (rule) and proportion, when the work is executed swiftly and surely.

6. Maniera (Manner) – The Style or Manner of an artist or school. The True and Fine style is the 'modern' style of Leonardo and Michelangelo (according to Vasari).

7. Rule – Rule or Measurement, is the measurement of antique statues and paintings, and basing modern works on these proportions or measurements.

8. Order - Order is the distinction of one style from another. Different styles should not be used together haphazardly. An example of Order includes the Ionic and Doric orders of ancient architecture.

9. Proportion - Proportion is the rule of correct alignment and proper arrangement. Objects were positioned partly using musical proportions, harmonic grids and geometry.

10. Design - Design is also considered as the imitation of the most beautiful in nature, used for the creation of all objects or figures and the ability of the artist to reproduce what he sees.

11. Fine Style - Fine Style is the use of the most beautiful and appropriate parts to produce a work of art.

Renaissance painting is usually linear, with defined outlines and forms that are evenly lit with no harsh shadows. It predominantly relies on a planar arrangement of the subject (objects are arranged on planes one behind the other which are parallel to the picture plane). There is not much diagonal movement of the subject into or out of the plane of the picture. Renaissance painting also uses distinct colour groups rather than a blended, merged and unified colour scheme.

Botticelli, *Madonna and Child*

Rules of Renaissance Composition

From studying the works of the great masters, certain 'rules of composition' have been formulated. Some of these rules apply to all types of paintings throughout history and are not just applicable to Renaissance art. These 'Rules of Composition' are rather to be considered as guidelines. They do not have to be strictly adhered to, there is room for artistic invention. Some or any of the 'rules' may be ignored in any one work. The following guidelines may be used to compose in the 'Renaissance style'.

1. Rule of Thirds
2. Groupings in Threes
3. Use of Geometric Shapes
4. Positioning objects using Musical Proportions
5. The use of Harmonic Grids
6. The use of Intriguing Outlines and Shapes
7. The use of Perspective
8. Use of the Diagonal to Divide the Canvas
9. Massing or Grouping of Colour Areas
10. The Golden Mean
11. Symmetry and Asymmetry
12. Use of Contrapposto

How to Apply the Rules

To apply the rules of Renaissance composition it is best to undertake a number of rough thumbnail sketches to work up your design. Once you have decided on a subject, such as a portrait, figure group or landscape, you should begin by considering the frame of the canvas. What are the proportions of the canvas you will be working on? The musical proportions 2:3 and 4:5 are common ratios for the sides of rectangular canvases. Consider how you will position the main subject within the frame. You may undertake several sketches to decide on a subject and to position the large shapes of the picture. The Rule of Thirds or the Golden Mean might form the basis for positioning your subject for example. For a figure group you may consider basing the overall figure group around a hidden geometric shape. Once you have determined a rough overall design for your main subject you may wish to overlay a harmonic grid (drawn in pencil with a ruler) and position the elements of the painting. You should spend some time considering the subject and thinking about what story or feeling lies behind the subject and choose appropriate objects and symbolism to best represent it. You might consider the foreground objects (your main subject) and then create a three dimensional space for the subject to occupy using perspective. Spotlight the prime focus by introducing high contrast of light against dark in that area and making the focus the brightest area of the painting or drawing. Don't produce just one sketch, make many variations to test out different ideas and arrangements. Choose the better compositions and consider each of the rules in turn and see if they can help to improve your composition. Once you have determined a composition, then proceed onto detailed study drawings of the key elements of the painting.

1. Rule of Thirds

Divide the canvas into three equal parts vertically and horizontally and place your subject according to the thirds.

(By the Author) Copy after Beccafumi, *Madonna*

The intersection points of the 'thirds grid' are considered important locations. These are known as the 'eyes of the canvas.' They may be used for locating the prime focus (the main subject of the painting) in an asymmetrical composition. Alternatively the thirds grid may be used to position the objects between the lines in a symmetrical arrangement (as above).

The Fibonacci Grid

Another set out grid, used in a similar way to 'the rule of thirds', is based on the Golden Mean ratio; it is known as the Fibonacci Grid.

The Fibonacci Grid is of the ratio: 1:0.618:1 on each side.

A simple method of laying out an approximate Fibonacci grid is to divide each side into eight parts and to draw horizontals and verticals at three and five on each side.

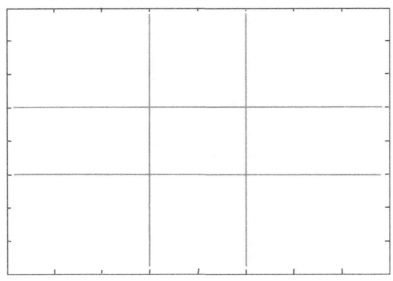

Rebatement of a Rectangle

Rebatement of a Rectangle is another method of dividing a rectangle to form a single square or two squares within the rectangle of the canvas. To find the Eyes of a canvas with Rebatement, draw the diagonals of the canvas. Where they cross the Lines of Rebatement are the locations of the eyes. The Lines of Rebatement are used to position important objects in the painting (such as the main subject) and to position strong vertical elements.

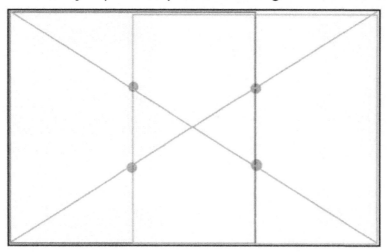

2. Groupings in threes

Group objects in threes to be unsymmetrical but balanced.

Leonardo Da Vinci, *The Last Supper.*

Group objects in threes or odd numbers. Try to have an odd number of objects rather than an even number.

Three is an important number in sacred geometry, representing the Holy Trinity, and is therefore considered as the number of Perfection.

3. Use Geometric shapes in the design of the composition

Use simple geometric shapes such as the triangle, pyramid, square, and circle.

Leonardo Da Vinci, *Virgin of the Rocks (Louvre)*

The Gestalt theory of composition allows the viewer to fill in the dots, sort of like seeing pictures in constellations of stars. You can suggest a geometrical shape in a picture by defining the vertices and/or parts of the sides with objects. You do not have to completely show the geometrical shape.

The Golden Triangle

One special triangle used in Renaissance painting is known as the Golden Triangle. This is an isosceles triangle with approximate proportions of base to height of 2:3 (forming angles of approximately 72 degrees, 36 degrees and 72 degrees at each vertex).

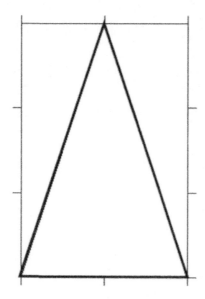

The Golden Triangle

4. Position objects using simple 'musical' proportions

Use 'musical proportions such as 1:2 (i.e. divide in half), 2:3 (i.e. divide 2/3rds to 1/3rd), 3:4 (divide at the 3/4 mark or 1/4 mark), 4:5 etc.

Botticelli, *Primavera*

Use the Musical Proportions or Golden Mean to divide the canvas and position objects. The spaces between shapes and objects should be made to be different from one another.

Musical Proportions are derived from the ancient musical theory of harmony that is said to have been discovered by Pythagoras the ancient Greek mathematician and philosopher. Pythagoras discovered a blacksmith working who produced certain harmonies with different weights of hammers on an anvil. He found that the weights of the harmonious hammers were of certain whole number ratios. From this discovery he formulated a theory of harmony based on these harmonious ratios. In a musical scale of an octave or eight notes, there are certain intervals (distances between two notes from the scale) which are harmonious. The intervals of the octave (8 notes), the perfect fifth (5 notes) and perfect fourth (4 notes) were

18

found to be the most harmonious when played together. Other intervals from the scale are less harmonious. The intervals of the octave, fifth and fourth were found to be related to the following mathematical ratios:

- Octave = 1:2
- Fifth = 2:3
- Fourth = 3:4

The ancient and medieval artists and philosophers considered that harmony in a painting could be obtained by using the musical proportions to position objects and to divide the canvas.

The ratio of 2:3 is most probably the more important as it is an approximation of the Golden Proportion (1:1.618)

The theory of musical ratios is given in the book, *The Fundamentals of Music by Boethius*, and was also applied to architectural proportion by the Greeks and Romans as recorded by the Roman architect, Vitruvius.

Giovanni Bellini, *Deposition*

5. Harmonic Grids

Use a harmonic grid to divide the canvas and position objects.

Various Harmonic Grids

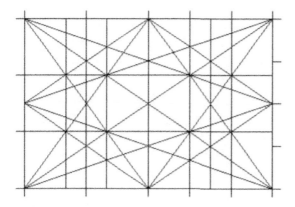

Armature of a Rectangle

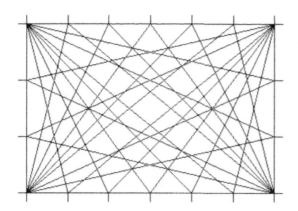

Sixths and Thirds

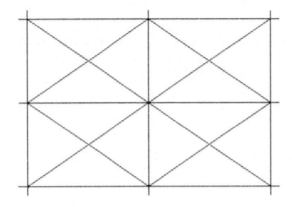

Half Grid and Diagonals

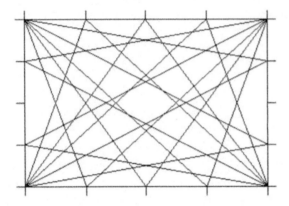

Quarters and two quarters

A harmonic grid is a means of dividing the canvas with lines based on nodal points positioned in accordance with harmonious musical proportions (and/or the golden mean). This grid is used as a guide in laying out the composition and in positioning and aligning objects in the painting.

Example of the use of a Harmonic Grid

Andrea Mantegna, *Parnassus (with Armature of a Rectangle)*

It is the intersection points of the diagonals which are most important in positioning your objects or subjects. The actual diagonal alignments are of lesser importance, though in some cases, as in this Mantegna painting, they form quite a strong element of the painting.

For more information relating to harmonic grids and the hidden geometry of art, I refer you to the book, *'The Painter's Secret Geometry' by Charles Bouleau.*

6. Use interesting shapes for your objects and negative spaces.

Uccello, *Battle of San Romano, Uffizi*

Use intriguing shapes of different sizes, not the same size, for variety. Having many objects creates interest and variation. However, do not create a confusion of shapes. Also consider the shape of the negative spaces. (Negative space is the space around or between objects). Interesting shapes are convoluted, with varying sized elements.

Uccello, *Head in a Roundel.*

7. Make use of perspective for the setting of the subject.

The subject should be placed within a 3-dimensional space (architectural space or landscape).

Raphael, *Marriage of the Virgin*

Objects get proportionally smaller as they get further away. Parallel lines going into the canvas converge to a vanishing point at the theoretical horizon. (Here, in Raphael's painting, the Vanishing Point is located at the doorway of the building).

Note the overlapping of the foreground figures. This is another form of perspective that implies that the figures are occupying a three dimensional space.

The use of atmospheric or colour perspective is also apparent in this painting. The tiling of the pavement in the middle-ground is a predominantly warm reddish colour. As we move into the background we move to cooler and less saturated colours, greens, blues, and pale blues of the background hills and sky.

The use of **Tiling** is a common Renaissance method of giving a sense of perspective or depth in a painting. The pattern of tiles becomes smaller as it recedes away from the viewer. This technique of using a receding tiling pattern is not limited to manmade floors or pavements, but may be applied to natural landscapes also. In landscapes you can create tiles from light and dark patches of grass, forest, or foliage (or from hedged fields) which diminish in size as they recede from the viewer.

Jan van Eyck, *The Rolin Madonna*

8. Use the diagonal in the composition of the subject to divide the canvas.

Titian, *Danae*

Diagonal composition is dynamic and suggests movement. Foreshortened diagonals into the canvas were used by Tintoretto and the Baroque masters. Renaissance diagonals are generally parallel to the picture plane.

9. Mass or group, colours and tones.

Use simple and limited colour schemes. The colour groups should have a balance over all the picture.

Durer, *Penitent St Jerome* (NB. This diagram is best viewed on a colour device).

10. Golden Mean

Use the Golden Mean in the composition or design of your painting.

Golden Rectangle

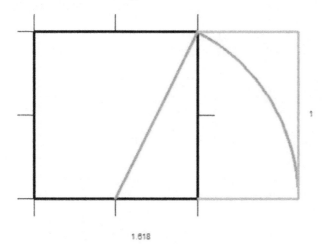

1.618

The golden rectangle has sides of a ratio of approximately 1:1.618. It is formed from a square and another smaller golden rectangle. The proportions of the golden rectangle are supposedly based on divine harmonious proportions in accordance with the sacred geometry of the universe.

The golden rectangle can be used as the format or frame of a painting. The golden mean ratio, 1:0.618, can also be used to subdivide the canvas and to position objects.

The golden rectangle can also be used as a geometrical shape within the picture, around which a composition may be based.

Fibonacci Grid

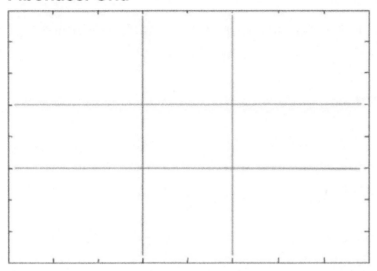

The Fibonacci Grid is of the ratio: 1:0.618:1 on each side. It is used in a similar manner to the 'rule of thirds' to layout objects on the canvas.

A simple method of laying out a Fibonacci grid is to divide each side into eight parts and to draw horizontals and verticals at 3 and 5 on each side.

Harmonics of the Golden Mean

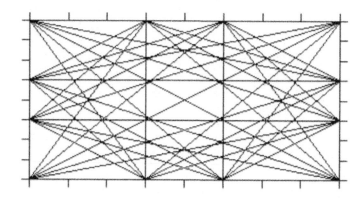

This is the Harmonic Grid based on the Golden Mean (approximately).

This harmonic grid is based around the Fibonacci Grid with added diagonals.

Golden Triangle

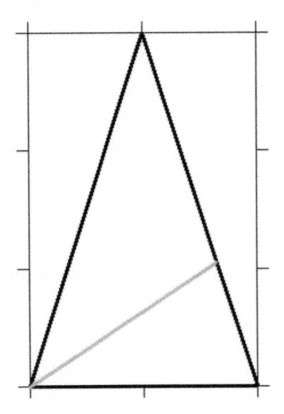

This is an isosceles triangle with approximate proportions of base to height of 2:3 (forming angles of approximately 72 degrees, 36 degrees and 72 degrees at each vertex).

The Golden Triangle can be subdivided to give another Golden Triangle by bisecting one of the base angles.

The Golden (or Fibonnaci) Spiral

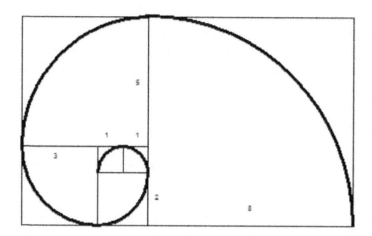

You can use the Golden Spiral or Fibonacci Spiral to position your prime focus at the centre of the spiral. The Golden Spiral is similar to the Fibonacci Spiral shown, except that the rectangle used is a Golden Rectangle rather than a sequence of squares based on the Fibonacci sequence, (1,1,2,3,5,8...etc.)

The Pentagon and Pentangle

The pentangle contains many Golden mean ratios in its construction. To draw the pentangle (five pointed star) you first need to draw a pentagon within a circle of the required dimension.

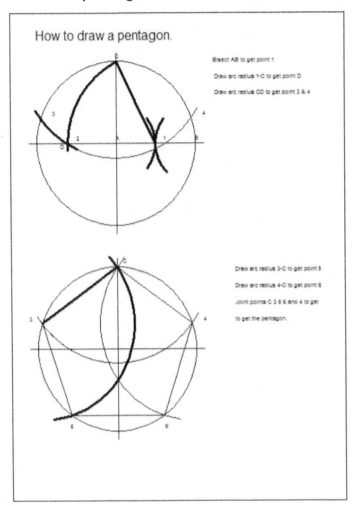

How to draw a pentagon.

Bisect AB to get point 1

Draw arc radius 1-C to get point D

Draw arc radius CD to get point 3 & 4

Draw arc radius 3-C to get point 5

Draw arc radius 4-C to get point 6

Joint points C 3 5 6 and 4 to get

to get the pentagon.

11. Symmetry and Asymmetry

Make use of Symmetry and Asymmetry according to the subject.

Leonardo da Vinci, *Mona Lisa*

A 'central' but asymmetrical composition was used in Leonardo da Vinci's, *Mona Lisa*.

Raphael, *School of Athens*

Raphael's, *School of Athens*, uses a large scale symmetry with small scale variations and asymmetry.

When considering the composition of a painting compare the two halves of the painting. You may have a symmetrical arrangement, but a strictly symmetrical arrangement is uninteresting. The symmetrical composition should be symmetrical on a large scale, but with variations of detail and asymmetry within the large scale symmetry.

The painting can also be unsymmetrical (but balanced), containing an active half (busy, lots of details) and a quieter passive half. As seen in Giorgione's, *The Three Philosophers*, (following).

A triangular and symmetrical composition denotes stability and authority and was often used in Church Paintings. More random and asymmetrical compositions were used in secular paintings.

Giorgione, *The Three Philosophers*

12. Contrapposto

Contrapposto (or turning of the parts) was often used to make figures in paintings graceful.

Leonardo da Vinci, *The Lady with the Ermine*

Cesare da Sesto after Leonardo, *Leda and the Swan*

In *The Lady with the Ermine* by Leonardo da Vinci, the lady's head faces one direction whilst her body faces another. Similarly the ermine's body is bent or turning in one direction and its head faces another.

With full length figures, the head, torso and legs, should all face in different directions and the line across the shoulders should be tilted in the opposite direction to the line of the hips. The weight of the figure should be predominantly supported on one leg. A typical contrapposto pose is shown in the painting of *Leda and the Swan*.

The Process of Composition and Painting in the Renaissance

The process that the Renaissance painters followed may have included:

- **Compositional sketches** (Quick gestural sketches to work out the overall position of objects, figures and limbs within the picture).
- **Detailed study drawings** (Detailed studies of key parts of the proposed painting. These should be well finished and rendered drawings).
- **Detailed Cartoon** (The Cartoon is a detailed drawing of the complete composition).
- **Colour Study** (A small study in colour to test the colour scheme for the painting).
- **The Final Painting** (The Final Painting was usually done using a Grisaille and Glazing method).

Compositional sketches

These were quick gestural sketches to work out the overall position of objects, figures and limbs within the picture, giving appropriate regard to the decorum of the gestures of figures to express the thought in the subject's mind.

Use 'Gesture sketching' to determine the composition and location of limbs and figures to express the mind of the subject in accordance with the Renaissance idea of 'Decoro'.

Maybe work out a scene in words and pictures to get an idea of the composition. Make up a story. Also create abstract doodles and stains, and collages to use as inspirations. Look at these patterns and see what they suggest to you. Do lots of doodling and scribbling.

Work in a light line and don't worry about finish until you have the limbs and figures positioned. Make use of Contrapposto to add Grace to your figures.

The states of mind of the figures may be based on the medieval concept of the four humours: Phlegmatic, Choleritic, Sanguineous, and Melancholic. Phlegmatic is a passive personality, a bit stuffy and aloof. Choleritic is an angry, abrasive and warlike personality. Sanguineous is of a jovial or excitable personality. Lastly, Melancholic is a sad and wistful personality. You could also use astrological zodiac personality types.

Keep a hardcover sketchbook for keeping ideas and doing thumbnail sketches for compositions. Work in two ways: in 'line', and in 'mass' (areas of light and dark). Work in monochrome at first, colour can come later. Keep the thumbnail sketches small, work out the main positions of the objects and pay attention to the negative spaces. Keep the shapes complex and interesting but not overly busy.

Think about:

- **Balance**: The image should look balanced even when seen in mirror image.
- **Rule of thirds**: Divide the canvas in thirds; and group objects in threes.
- **Proportions**: Use the golden mean or musical proportions to position objects and to divide a canvas into varying sized parts. Use the 'Canon of Human Proportions' as a guide for drawing the human figure.
- **Contrast**: Provide a strong contrast at the prime focus of the painting. (Light on Dark, or Dark on Light).
- **Prime Focus**: Concentrate all you effort on the prime focus, then on the secondary and tertiary foci. All lines should lead to or frame the prime focus.
- **Secondary Focus**: The prime focus should direct the viewer to the secondary focus. Such as by the use of line

or edge pointing to it, or having a figure looking back or gesturing to the secondary focus.

- **Geometric Shapes:** Use the triangle or other simple geometric shapes to design the picture around.
- Initially concentrate on line and tone for composition, colour comes later.
- Work with the overall large shapes first and the frame of the canvas to compose your picture (forget the details for the moment, the details can be dealt with later).

Getting ideas

Ideas and inspiration come from: scenes from nature and life, doodling and spontaneous sketching, dreams and visions, books, poems and stories, and other paintings. The Renaissance artist drew inspiration from the stories of the Bible and from Ovid's 'Metamorphoses'. I suggest buying a copy of 'Bulfinch's Mythology' if you are interested in the mythological subjects. The subject is not necessarily important; other than the artist should have an empathy with it, and the subject should be interesting.

The artist should aim for a feeling or emotion such as: love, beauty, calm, serenity, awe, vitality, vibrancy, a religious, spiritual and emotional feeling, the numinous mystery. Art should not necessarily be ugly for its own sake. The subject should be chosen to suite these feelings.

Keep a sketchbook for ideas.

Some subjects/ideas

Landscapes (and nature) have elements of awe and the sublime: majestic mountains, dark mysterious grottoes, murky woods, glowing spring light, peaceful forest glades, sunset and mysterious twilight, fluffy white clouds, towering thunderstorms, stars and galaxies, fire, lightning, ocean waves, wind, tornadoes, typhoons, snowy landscapes. Strange rock formations, rocks shaped like people, towering clouds and storm fronts, waterfalls and cliffs, caves with stalactites and stalagmites, mysterious mists, anything awesome and awe inspiring, thermal springs, ice bergs, bush fires, volcanoes, waterfalls and streams. Include figures in the landscape to give a sense of scale.

Love is conveyed by beauty (usually but not always): mother and child, noble youths, pure maidens, the Graces.

Animals: Such as birds in flight, angels and winged horses, majestic and fearsome lions, colourful parrots and birds of paradise, noble and graceful horses (power and movement), friendly and vicious dogs, fantastic beasts and wild animals.

Ancient architecture: Architectural wonders, spires and towers, domes and arches, old and futuristic, castles, cathedrals, sailing ships. More modern equivalents might include: steam trains and ships, majestic zeppelins and airships, graceful balloons, archaic biplanes, sleek rockets and jets, spacemen and spaceships, complex radio antennae and electrical pylons and substations with insulators, complex computers and printed circuit boards, trains, planes and automobiles.

Faerie: Elves, witches, wizards and druids, dragons, dwarves, phoenixes and other fantastic birds, goblins, demons and devils, angels, ghosts, gods and goddesses and mythological beasts.

People: Nobles, knights, beautiful nudes, mother and child (love and serenity), peasants, skulls and skeletons, saints,

Leonardo da Vinci, *Sketch for Leda and the Swan*

Leonardo da Vinci, *Sketch for a Monument with Horse and Rider*

Detailed study drawings

Detailed studies were done for key parts of the proposed painting. These should be well drawn and rendered with regard to proportion, and light and shade (chiascuro). Do detailed study drawings of parts of the composition such as trees, leaves, faces, hands, feet, anatomy, props, and draperies. Get as much detail, accuracy and shading, as you can in the sketches. You can take reference photos of details which may be of use to the composition but try to get the lighting consistent to suit the light source in the painting.

When drawing figures from life draw the overall pose quickly and lightly. Then do a study of the most interesting part of the pose; for example, it may be the hands, feet, draperies or face etc.

Questions that the Artist should ask when doing a study from life:

- How many? Quantify!
- Where? Locate!
- What Shape? Proportions!
- What Colour? Tone! Hue!
- Why is it so?

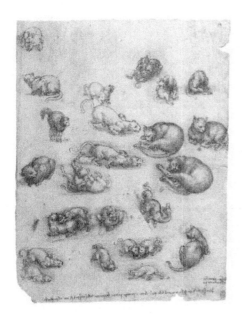

Leonardo da Vinci, *Study of Cats*

Leonardo da Vinci, *Study of St. Paul for the Last Supper*

Detailed Cartoon

The Cartoon was a large detailed drawing of the complete composition, usually at the full size of the final painting. This enabled an artist to test out the composition and get it correct before transferring the drawing to a canvas or panel. Cartoons should be finished works of art in their own right.

Leonardo da Vinci, *The Burlington House Cartoon.*

Colour Study

This would be a simple small study in colour to test and determine the colour scheme for the painting. The massing and locating of colour within the painting was considered. Do small colour sketches in pastel, watercolour or oils to work out the major colour harmony of the painting. The coloured painting needs to be harmonious and balanced.

The Venetian painters used very strong and luminous colours, full of light and vibrancy. Florentine Renaissance painters used more subdued colours with occasional bright highlights of key colours like red, white, yellow or blue.

In the Renaissance colour theory the colours were classified into groups according to their elemental nature. Alberti calls these groups Genera (families). The Genera of colour are the hues. There are four Genera according to Alberti:

- Red (Fire)
- Blue (Air)
- Green (Water)
- Ash (Grey or Brown) (Earth)

The Species of colour are made by adding black or white to the Genera

Leonardo says there are six main colours including black and white. These are (from lightest to darkest):

- white (All),
- yellow (earth),
- green (water),
- blue (air),
- red (fire),
- black (void).

Leonardo also goes on to say that: green goes well with red, purple or violet, and that blue goes well with yellow

White and Yellow add gaiety, and dark colours lend sobriety. Red lends a sensual and fiery nature. Blue, calm and melancholy. Purple is regal.

When applying colours on a painting you should intersperse the light colours, white and yellow, with the darker colours, blue, red, green and black to create contrast and variety. You should go for a variety of colours arranged harmoniously. Alberti gives the example of: green beside white, beside red, beside yellow.

Balance the colours over the painting. If you have a red on the left of the painting, then you should balance it with another red on the right hand side of the canvas etc.

The Final Painting

Sketch the composition on the canvas lightly in charcoal; or transfer it from the cartoon using: tracing, gridding, or pricking and pouncing. Get the position of the major shapes and outlines. Go over the charcoal drawing and fix it with ink or paint. Fill in the major shadows. Decide on a suitable painting technique, tempera, under-painting and glazing in oils (Northern, Venetian or Leonardo technique). Allow the composition to change or vary according to the dictates of the painting. The final composition could be altered and changed according to the judgement of the painter. Renaissance paintings in oils were usually done using a Grisaille and Glazing method or similar.

Transfer Techniques

A tracing technique, suggested by Vasari in his treatise, *On Technique*, for transferring cartoons non-destructively to a panel or canvas is to create a sheet of transfer paper using a sheet of thin paper covered well with charcoal on the back. Place this paper, charcoal side face down on the canvas, underneath the cartoon to be traced. Hinge the cartoon to the canvas or panel using masking tape (Vasari suggests nails or pins) so that you may lift and replace the cartoon and transfer paper without shifting it out of position on the canvas. This allows you to check on the progress of your tracing.

Trace over the cartoon, pressing firmly, using a smooth, hard stylus (such as a paper embossing tool or the end of a paintbrush handle). This will transfer the lines of the drawing, in charcoal onto the canvas.

Concerning Proportion

Canon of Human Proportions

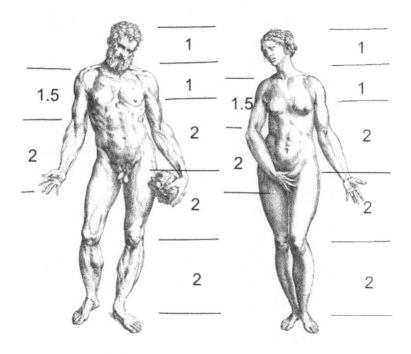

Proportions of a man and woman.

The Canon of Human Proportions is a guide to drawing the human figure in proportion. It originated in the Ancient world, Greece and Egypt had their own Canons of Proportion and the Roman writer on architecture, Vitruvius wrote down a Canon of Human proportion. In Renaissance times Leonardo da Vinci formulated a Canon of Proportion, as did Albrecht Durer.

The Canon for the human figure given above is based on a height of the figure equal to 8 head lengths. The length of the head is the reference length equal to one unit. To layout a standing figure, mark the positions of the top of the head and the bottom of the feet. Then divide this in half by eye, and then further divide these halves to get quarters. Divide the top quarter to get eighths, (the size of the head).

The quarter points give the: top of the crown, the nipples of the male, the groin, the knees, and the bottom of the feet.

You should remember that the Canon of Proportion is only a guide. People vary in proportion, some are tall, others fat, some are short, and others skinny. Men, women and children of different ages are all of different proportions.

Proportions of a 5 year old Child

The overall height of a 5 year old child is about 5/8ths of an adult male. The child's head is 1/6th of its body length. The proportions of the limbs and body are similar to an adult allowing for the difference in head size.

Proportions of a 1 year old Baby

The overall height of a 1 year old baby is about 3/8ths of an adult male. The baby's head is 1/4th of its body length. The proportions of the limbs and body are similar to an adult but are a bit chubbier (allowing for the difference in head size).

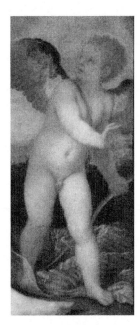

Titian, *Details of Danae*

Titian, *Detail of The Worship of Venus.*

Proportions of the Head.

Determine the top and bottom (height) of the head according to the Canon of Human Proportions and then the sides (width) of the head. Check the proportion of the width to the height is correct. You can start by drawing a simple oval shape and using construction straight lines. Once you have the outline of the head you can position a horizontal centreline for both eyes, usually half way between the top and bottom of the head.The position of this eyeline will be affected by the orientation of the head Then draw the edge of the nose. In a three-quarter view you only draw one side of the nose (the edge away from you). Draw a line of the cheek bone or edge of shadow at the cheek bone to help define the shape of the head. The mouth is not straight, the top lip projects down in the middle. The mouth is a bit like a very shallow M shape. To position the eyes, end of the nose, and mouth, use the *proportions of the head* (see following diagram).

Drawing the head in proportion

To draw the shape of the head in proportion fairly accurately from a reference photo or model, draw a square around the face on the reference photo (or use a square viewing frame cut out of paper when looking at a live model). Then draw the square on your canvas in the location and size that you want the head to appear. As long as the square is well proportioned then your face proportions, drawn using construction lines within the square should come out in the right width to height ratio. This method relies on judgement of the eye not measuring and tracing through mechanical gridding and copying.

Diagram: Drawing the head in proportion using a square frame.

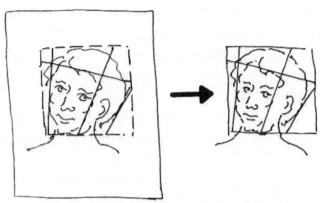

Drawing the Head in Proportion

Proportions of the head

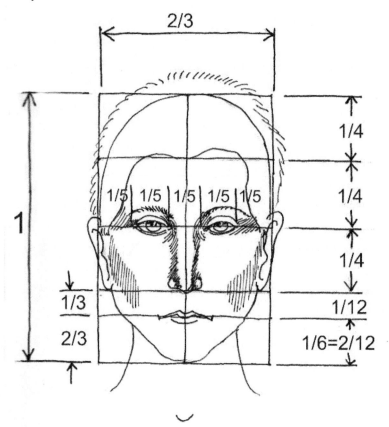

The Proportions of the Face

Begin with the eyes and nose. The eye-line is located half way between the crown of the head and the bottom of the chin. The eyes are generally 1/5th of the width of the head with one eye-width between them. So divide the front of the face eye-line into five equal segments. Draw the shape of the eyes copying the shape closely from your reference or sitter. Use triangulation, angles and similar lengths to position and draw the features of the face. Use verticals and horizontals from key features to check the locations of lines and to relate lines. Don't be afraid to rub out incorrect lines. (Hint: Draw the new line before you rub out the old line, so you don't repeat your mistake). Remember the face is a curved surface. The eyelids and lips may curve or wrap around the curved form of the face. Don't forget to positon the ear correctly. The top of the ear generally lines up with the top of the top eyelid and the bottom of the ear with the bottom of the nose.

Key triangulation points to check when drawing the face.

Shading the Form of the Head

When drawing and shading the figure or objects consider the features as simple solid forms such as the cylinder, sphere, and cube.

  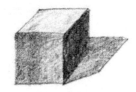

There is a hierarchy of forms in the figure:

- The limb or body.
- The muscles and features.
- Wrinkles and veins

The secondary forms should be subservient to the overall form of the head, body or limb.

Shade the body with regard to the: 1. primary shadow, 2. reflected light, 3. main light, 4. highlight, and 5. cast shadow.

Different Shaped Noses

flat   hooked   snub   concave   straight/aqualine   convex

The form of the head and the features of the face must be defined by light and shade. A fixed light source, generally from one direction should be used to accentuate the form of the face. A good example of Renaissance shading of form is given by the works of Leonardo da Vinci (see the angels head below). Surface planes facing the light source are the brightest and those facing away are darkest (except where reflected light on the jaw illuminates the edge).

The top of the forehead is bright.

Under the eyebrows is dark, especially near the bridge of the nose. The top eyelid is light. The lower eyelid is in shadow.

The edge of the shadow on the cheek of the face is defined by the shape of the cheek bone.

The top lip is generally in shadow and the bottom lip is lighted. Under the bottom lip is cast in shadow.

Light reflected from the shoulder illuminates the edge of the jaw line and gives a realistic three dimensional form.

The features of the head can be related to simple forms when determining shading. The front of the nose is like a cylinder, the nostril is like a sphere. The head as a whole can be shaded like a sphere or a block depending on the shape of the head. The whole of the eye, including upper and lower eyelids, is sort of like a sphere sunken into the head.

A three quarter view (from the side and the front) gives the easiest way to see and draw the form of the head and its features. (Much easier than a directly front-on view).

The light source could be from either the right or left side. Generally a light source on the side facing the face is easiest to shade (as in Leonardo's painting).

Practice

Practice drawing the layout of a head and face until you get into a habit of drawing the face with the proportions close to correct. Don't worry about getting a likeness initially. Just practice drawing hundreds of small faces. Each face has a life of its own. One tip is to make sure you draw a happy face with a sweet smile. Faces can have habit of becoming sad and melancholic. Be careful of sad drooping eyes and frowning lips unless you deliberately mean to do these. Draw faces lots and lots. Don't draw just beautiful pop and movie stars. Draw interesting faces, old people with lots of wrinkles, faces with a lot of character.

(You can check out many videos on drawing faces on YouTube. The Youtube channel by, 'Alphonso Dunn', has good tutorials on drawing figures, faces, and other subjects. Alphonso has also written a book, *"Pen and Ink Drawing" by Alphonso Dunn*, available on Amazon.com).

The Proportions of the Hand

The overall size of the hand (from the heel of the palm to the tip of the middle (long) finger is the same size as the persons face. (From the chin to the hair line, roughly ¾ of a head length).

To draw the hand in proportion, indicate the rough size of the overall hand and then draw the palm (or back of the hand) first. It is approximately a square, slightly lengthened to be rectangular in the direction of the length of the hand. It is very slightly shorter than half the length of the overall hand with the fingers straight.

The four knuckles at the top of the back of the palm lie on a curve with the long finger's knuckle being highest. Locate the knuckle of the longest (middle) finger. The long finger is the same length as from the wrist to the knuckle plus the length of the fingernail. The first joint in the finger is halfway between the knuckle and the base of the nail. The next joint lies about halfway between the first joint and the tip of the finger.

The length of the index finger comes to the level of the base of the fingernail of the long finger.

The ring finger is about the same length as the index finger or just slightly longer. The joints of the fingers lie along a steeper arc than the knuckles of the palm.

The knuckle of the thumb is halfway up the palm of the hand and offset to the side of the palm. The joint of the thumb is level with the knuckle of the index finger. The tip of the thumb comes midway between the knuckle and first joint of the index finger. The fingernail of the thumb is at 90 degrees to the fingernails of the other fingers.

The fingers can be shaded as cylinders. Between the fingers is generally dark and in shadow. The back of the hand contains details such as tendons and veins. Do not overstate these, be subtle.

Proportions
of the Hand

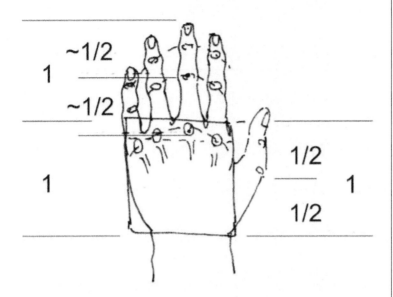

~1/2

1

~1/2

1

1/2

1

1/2

The rectangle of the palm
is slightly longer than it
is wide.

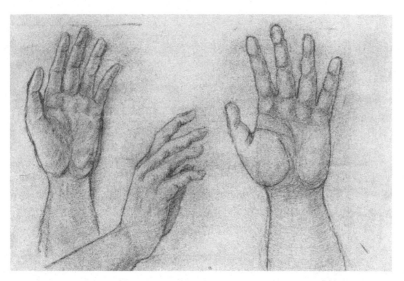

By the Author, *Study of Hands – Silverpoint*

Arranging of Figures

Compositional Sketching of Figures

It is recommended to join a life drawing group at your local art centre. There are life drawing internet resources on 'YouTube' if you don't have access to a life drawing group. Sketch the poses of the figures and do detailed studies of the most interesting part of the pose such as the head, torso, hands or feet. Do a number of different poses from the same life model on the one sheet of paper and try to arrange these in interesting compositions. You can use these drawings as references to come up with your own compositions.

Work out the arrangement of figures and groups by doing a number of compositional sketches concentrating on the large shapes and major limbs of the figures. Find an arrangement that you like.

Proportion

Use the Canon of Human Proportions as a guide to producing your human figures, but only as a guide. You should adjust the proportions using your own artistic judgement. Real people do not fit strictly into the Canon of Proportions, they come in all shapes and sizes. The proportions of the human body vary with age and gender.

Decorum

Decorum is the appropriateness of gesture, expression, clothing and setting. The gestures of the figure or figures should reflect their mind and show what they are thinking. This idea of decorum should be reflected even down to the details like the fingers and toes.

Decorum also applies to the appropriateness of the limbs of the figures. The limbs and features should match the body to which they are attached. A short stout bodied person should not have long thin limbs and vice versa. The head of an old person should not be placed on a youthful body.

To show **Love**: use a beautiful smiling face with happy or dreamy eyes and a relaxed graceful expression. The figure should have gentle, smooth and glowing skin and refined delicate and graceful hands.

To show **Anger**: The expression has a furrowed nose and brow and mean slitted eyes, an angry grimace of the mouth, a sneer, tense limbs and muscles in forceful gestures. The hands will be clenched or tense, also the toes. The veins will be standing out.

To show **Joy**: A happy, laughing, smiling face, clapping or relaxed hands, and sparkling eyes. A pose showing relaxed movement.

To show **Sadness**: A sad face with downturned mouth or pouting lip. Tearful drooping eyes, the brow furrowed with anguish, the head downcast or else turning to heaven, the hands clutching at the garments, or covering the face, or clutching the head. The body sagging and shoulders hunched.

Grace

In keeping with Decorum of a figure is Grace. A softness, facility and appropriateness. A calmness or gentleness of expression. The gestures and movements of figures should not be overstated or harsh. To endow the figures with grace use the techniques of Contrapposto (turning of the parts of a figure in different directions) and avoid stiffness in the pose by having the limbs bent at all the joints: The shoulder, elbow and wrist, the hip, knee and ankle, even down to the fingers and toes.

Extend the gracefulness to the clothes or drapes, with appropriate graceful folding or crumpling. Do not have many harsh folds cutting across the form of the figure or limbs.

Have graceful, long, curly or wavy hair.

Botticelli, *Detail from Primavera*

Clothes

Clothes should be of a universal or old fashioned style as seen in the paintings of the great masters. Set up drapes over chairs or a mannequin and draw studies of the drapes from life. Take account of the nature of the cloth, thick with a few large folds, or thin with many small folds, and consider how tight fitting the cloth is. Loose cloth has free flowing curved folds. Tight fitting cloth has straighter, taut folds, running in the direction of tension.

Arranging figures in groups

Arrange your figures around a hidden geometry. Use simple geometric shapes such as the triangle, square or circle. The geometry could be symbolic in nature as in 'sacred geometry'.

Have one figure as a prime focus. This figure may be 'spotlighted' against a contrasting background.

Arrange the limbs in line with decorum, the idea in the mind of each figure. Also position the figures and limbs to create intriguing negative shapes between and around the figures.

Angling

Use angling of the figures, that is, the tilt and turn of adjacent figures and limbs in different directions to create acute angles, like the vertexes of a triangle. Face the fronts of figures in different directions.

The figures should preferably be angled to each other in all three dimensions. That is: Vertically (inclined across the picture plane), Horizontally (twisting, turning or facing), and in Depth (inclination into the picture plane). The following diagram gives an example of 'Angling' of three objects.

Example: Angling of Blocks

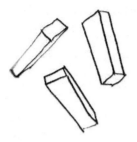

Example: Angling of People

Rhythmic Horizontal Positioning

In a horizontal arrangement of figures you should rhythmically vary the spacing of figures to add interest to the picture group. This can be considered like a piece of music with long and short beats.

Example of Rhythmic Variations in Horizontal Positioning

You may overlap figures to create larger unified groups.

Symbolism

Include props in your scene or with your figures that are symbolic in meaning. Buy a 'Dictionary of Symbology' for reference. Various animals, flowers and objects have symbolic meanings. Make sure the symbology is appropriate to the decorum of your painting's subject.

Examples of symbolism include: roses for love, a candle or lamp for enlightenment, a lily for death, A lion for savage nobility (the lion is also a symbol for Christ in religious paintings), an apple for knowledge or forbidden fruits, etc.

Albrecht Durer, *Melancholia 1*

The Size of Figures

The size of the main figures in a painting should be in proportion to the size of the canvas and the requirements of the genre.

For example: If you are painting a landscape the prime focus should be on a feature of the landscape, a cloud, mountain, tree, or lake, etc. Figures should be appropriately small so as to not draw undue attention from the prime focus. The figures in the landscape can become a secondary or tertiary focus to give a sense of scale to the landscape.

Joachim Patinir,
Landscape with St. Jerome in a Cave

If the main subject of a painting is a figure or group of figures, then those figures should be appropriately large to dominate the scene. Usually in a Figure painting the height of the figure or group will be at least half the height of the canvas or more.

Cesare da Sesto after Leonardo da Vinci,
Leda and the Swan

Leonardo da Vinci, *Virgin of the Rocks (London)*

Raphael, *The School of Athens*

If the subject is a portrait, the figure should be large enough that the facial features are recognisable. Generally the subject will fill a large area of the canvas whether it is a full length portrait or only the head.

Albrecht Durer, *St Jerome*

Brush work

Brushwork in Renaissance paintings is not very apparent as it is generally of a smooth and blended appearance, only textured where appropriate to suggest foliage, fur, hair, rock etc.

In the early renaissance a more linear painting style with sharp outlines and well defined edges and shapes was used. This was the case for the Florentine and Northern painters. The Venetian painters adopted a looser style with softer edges. Leonardo da Vinci invented the sfumato technique with soft smoky edges and no hard lines.

Botticelli, *Venus and Mars.*

Leonardo da Vinci's paintings seem to have looser brushwork in the atmospheric landscapes. (See the background of the *Mona Lisa* for example). This helps to lend a mysterious misty quality to the landscapes.

Leonardo da Vinci, *Detail of the Mona Lisa.*

Oil Painting Techniques

Materials

Renaissance Materials

The following pigments were commonly used in Renaissance times:

- White – lead white (toxic)
- Earths – ochres, umbers and siennas (raw and burnt)
- Yellow – lead-tin yellow (toxic), yellow ochre and Naples Yellow, and possibly saffron.
- Red – vermillion (toxic), Red Ochre, Red Lake
- Blue – Ultramarine, Azurite, Indigo and Smalt
- Green – Malachite and Verdigris
- Black – Bone black and charcoal

The use of many of these Renaissance pigments is not recommended especially the toxic ones.

Oils used included Linseed and Walnut oil. They also used egg (either egg yolk or whole egg) as a medium for tempera and tempera grassa (egg-oil).

The paint brushes used in the Renaissance were mainly round brushes made with hogs bristle, squirrel and fine sable.

Modern Materials

Oil Paints:

The following is a list of suggested modern pigments:

- Titanium White
- Burnt Sienna
- Raw Umber
- Burnt umber
- Yellow Ochre or Raw Sienna
- Chrome Yellow Pale or Cadmium Yellow Pale
- Cadmium Red

- Alizarin Crimson
- Ultramarine Blue
- Cobalt Blue
- Viridian
- Ivory Black

Medium:

- Refined Artist Linseed Oil; and
- Artist Spirit of Turpentine (or Odourless Solvent)

Use a 50%/50% mix of the above (oil/turps) for your painting medium.

You may also like to use a specialty Glazing medium, such as Art Spectrum No.4 Liquol or Winsor and Newton Liquin (Fine detail, or Glazing and blending medium).

Brushes:

Buy good quality bristle brushes. 3 or 4 of each size: Small, Medium, Large (4 to 15 mm in size). Filberts are best for starters, though Renaissance artists would have used rounds. Get a few (one or two) very small (No.0 or No.1 size round) synthetic or sable brushes for fine work.

Mahl stick:

A mahl stick or a wooden bridge is necessary to steady the brush hand when painting fine detail. You can make a mahl stick from a piece of 9mm wooden dowel, of an appropriate length, glued into a hole drilled into a small polystyrene ball (30mm dia.) available from art and craft supply shops.

The mahl stick is held in the left, or off, hand, and the ball end is rested gently on the backing board or canvas. The stick is used as a rest for the brush hand to keep the paintbrush steady whilst painting fine details.

Palette Cups:

It is suggested having two palette cups, of the type that can clip onto the side of a palette. One for turps and one for medium. You may get away with one for medium for starters. The palette cups should be separate, not joined, so you can easily pour unused medium and turps back into metal-lidded storage jars.

Palette:

Use a medium to large square or oval (kidney) palette. Wood or plastic.

You can make a cheap disposable palette from cardboard sealed with PVA wood glue.

Palette Knives:

You will need two palette knives, such as a small and medium trowel type palette knives. Buy the more expensive palette knives, not the cheapest ones. They must have very flexible and springy blades. The cheap ones are not so springy and flexible as they are made of an inferior grade of steel. The palette knife is used for mixing oil paint and cleaning paint off the palette. Renaissance painters did not usually use the palette knife for applying paint to the canvas.

Rags:

A rag or cloth for cleaning brushes and palette knives whilst working. Terry-towel tea towel is ideal. Paper towel can also be used for cleaning of palettes etc.

Use a **Metal Bin** for disposing used or messy paper towels or rags. **(NOTE: Oily Rags and papers can be a combustion hazard. They may spontaneously ignite. Dispose of safely).**

Aluminium foil:

This is used for covering your paint pigments on your palette to keep them from drying hard, whenever you leave your palette for an extended time (i.e. more than an hour or two). When you wish to leave off painting, tear off small squares of foil and press gently over your blob of pigment. Then seal around the edge of the paint by scribing around the foil over the edge of the pigment with the end of a paintbrush handle. This will seal the majority of the pigment from the air. Foil is better than plastic as it also protects the pigment from light (photoreactions). Pigment kept on a palette covered this way can last for months; this prevents wasting pigments by clearing off your palette after each session.

Easel:

If you are painting small pictures (16" x 20" or less) a simple table easel is a good affordable choice. Avoid working flat on the table, use an easel as this makes it easier to reach the vertical canvas or paper and is less restrictive on your gestures and arm movement whilst painting.

Later when you progress to larger paintings you can buy a larger easel.

Canvas, panel, paper, or cardboard:

These are the support or surface for your painting. Oil paint applied directly on paper or cardboard is not permanent, the paint and paper will deteriorate. The paper will soak up oil from the paint and the paints will flake off after a year or so. If you wish to save your work on paper, you can seal the paper, with PVA wood glue, or size or gelatine, prior to painting. In this case you may wish to use a heavier water-colour paper or cardboard to prevent buckling and wrinkling of the paper when being sealed. Alternatively, buy a prepared oil painting paper pad from the art store.

Linen canvas is preferred over cotton, but more expensive. Masonite (hardboard) panels prepared with acrylic gesso provide a good smooth surface suited to fine detail. Traditionally panels and canvases were prepared with a animal glue size and a glue or oil based gesso. Modern painters now use an acrylic gesso.

Other things you may need:
- A pencil for making notes.
- A table for setting up your desktop easel.

- A plastic sheet or tablecloth for protecting the table.
- A jar or two, with watertight metal cap, for saving medium and turps so it may be reused later.
- Two tins, one for turps for cleaning brushes and one as a stand for brushes not being used.
- A seat or stool if you wish to sit whilst painting.

Northern Oil Painting Technique

In the Northern Renaissance oil painting technique the support is usually a wooden panel, sized with animal skin glue and coated with a glue and chalk gesso ground. Then an underdrawing is prepared. A preliminary drawing is done in black chalk or charcoal on the gesso layer. The final underdrawing is done on the gesso layer with black paint (usually egg tempera), or ink, applied with pen or brush. Over this is laid an isolation layer of oil (linseed oil or walnut oil) to reduce the absorbency of the ground, possibly containing a lead drying agent. Sometimes this layer may also contain a reddish pigment.

A simple modern method to emulate this technique would be to use an acrylic gesso and do the underdrawing directly on the dry acrylic gesso with black acrylic paint.

Then the dead colours are applied. These were usually done using a medium consisting of oil with lead dryer and protein (egg). (See egg-oil emulsions in Appendix 3). The colour of the dead layer depends on the final colour of the object to be painted, for example:

- Blue – Underpainting (dead layer) is done with light blue. The final glaze is pure Ultramarine.
- Red – Underpainting is done in a light red (red with white). A second coat of underpainting is done in a darker light red. The glaze is with deep red.
- Green – The underpainting is done in grey tones. A second layer is done in light green). The glaze is with pure green.

You can substitute equivalent and safer modern oil paint pigments for the obsolete Renaissance pigments.

The first layers of the underpainting are done somewhat grey with some of the final colour. The second layer of underpainting is done with more of the final colour and is more transparent. Finally a thin glaze of pure colour, using a medium of pure oil with no egg binder, is applied. No white is used in the glazes.

Albrecht Durer, *Unfinished Salvatore Mundi*

Example of an underdrawing

Jan van Eyck, *St Barbara*

A finished, painted and glazed painting

Jan van Eyck, *Madonna in the Church*

The following is an example of a modern method based on the Northern Technique:

An underpainting (grisaille) in acrylic paint.

Filling in the flesh tones with oil paint.

The final painting with glazes in oil colours.

(By the Author, *The Witch*).

Venetian Grisaille

Venetian Oil Painting technique is a method of painting with glazes, that is thin transparent layers of colour, and is usually done over a tonal, mainly black and white and grey, underpainting known as a 'grisaille'. The Grisaille painting must be done in oils, in full detail and finished and left to dry completely (at least a week, possibly two weeks in colder weather) before the glazes are applied. Keep the Grisaille painting fairly light in tone as you are relying on the luminosity of the light areas to reflect light back through the transparent coloured glazes.

The Three Stages of Painting with Grisaille and Glazing

1. Underdrawing

By the Author, *Harpy*

The underdrawing should be sketched in loosely in oils and the main darks and lights indicated. Here, the ground has been tinted with a warm tone (Burnt Sienna). The drawing has been done in Ivory Black and the highlights scumbled in with Titanium White (working wet in wet).

2. Grisaille

The Grisaille is a fully refined underpainting done in mainly black and white grey-tones. This painting should be fully finished and left to completely dry (about 2 weeks) before applying the transparent glazes of colour over the top. An Ivory Black and Titanium White mix was used. It is alright for the coloured ground to show through in select places.

3. Glazing

Here we have the application of transparent glazes of colour over the grey underpainting. The glaze is oil paint highly diluted with glazing medium. You should use two or three layers of glaze and let each one dry between coats. This enables you to build up rich intense and luminous colours. You should try to apply the glazes smoothly without apparent brush strokes. Final highlights were done in Titanium White.

Transparent Paints for Glazing

You should mainly use transparent pigments for the glazes. I use the following artist quality transparent paints for glazing:

- Ultramarine Blue
- Viridian
- Transparent Yellow
- Scarlet Lake
- Alizarin

With these transparent colours I also use, highly diluted with medium, the following semi-opaque and opaque colours:

- Yellow Ochre (semitransparent)
- Cobalt Blue (semi opaque)
- Cadmium Red (opaque)
- Titanium White (opaque) (Used as a 'scumble') (possibly Zinc white could be better for glaze mixing/tinting though there are concerns about its reactivity and permanence)
- Ivory Black (semitransparent)

You should use 'artist quality' paints for glazing, not the cheaper student colours. You are relying on the high pigment concentration of the artist quality paint to provide the tinting power when the paint is highly diluted with glazing medium.

You can use a glazing medium, such as Winsor and Newton Liquin (use either Liquin Fine Detail or Blending and Glazing Medium) or Art Spectrum Liquol (Medium No.4), for diluting the paint. These contain alkyd varnish as well as oil and dryers to enhance drying time. You can also glaze using a standard 50/50 medium of linseed oil and artist turpentine but the glaze will take longer to dry. It is better to apply a slightly stronger tint of glaze than required. If the glaze colour is too strong the still wet glaze can be lifted gently off the surface of the painting with a clean rag to achieve the desired intensity.

I also find that using a white surfaced palette for mixing the transparent paints allows me to judge the colour of the transparent mix better. Transparent glazes of colour act to modify the underlying base colour. Hence, putting a blue glaze over yellow will give a green colour. Red over yellow will give an orange, and so on.

The Venetian painter's placed a strong emphasis on bright colours that were harmoniously arranged and balanced across the painting. Notable examples you should look at are works by the Bellini's, Giorgione and Titian (amongst others).

Titian, *Bacchus and Ariadne*

Leonardo's Painting Technique

Leonardo da Vinci was a great experimenter and used different painting techniques over his career. The following information relates to his usual method of painting panels (or sometimes canvases) and is drawn from various books (including Leonardo's treatise), and from information available on the internet.

1. Do your compositional sketches.

2. Do detailed studies for the key elements of the painting

3. Do a full sized detailed Cartoon

4. Prepare your canvas or panel with a ground. Leonardo seems to have used a warm ground made from lead white and Naples yellow.

5. Transfer the Cartoon to the Canvas using charcoal by copying using gridding, tracing, or pricking and pouncing to get the main outlines and proportions. Or redraw the composition whilst improving it.

6. Fix the light charcoal drawing by painting over it with dark paint such as thinned raw umber or ivory black oil paint. This thin greenish or brownish drawing is known as 'Verdaccio'. Shade in the main darks. Wait until dry.

7. Rub the charcoal away after the paint is dry.

8. Put on a yellowish colour intonaco (imprimatura) ground. Then apply a thin scumble of white to soften the lines. Make corrections where necessary. Let dry

9. Paint the underpainting in dead colours (pale versions of the final colours) Paint the lights first and then the darks. Model surfaces with lights and darks. Continue modelling in layers, building up semitransparent layers of colour, smoothing and blending to achieve sfumato (soft edges) where appropriate.

10. Then glaze with transparent colours to build up the colour intensity as required.

Leonardo used the following colours for flesh tones:

- Make the lights of the flesh tones with white, yellow and a little red.
- Paint the shadows of the flesh tones with white, black and red oxide (such as burnt sienna).

Leonardo used glazes of colour over dead colours (pale versions of the final colours). He also used a lake (red lake) pigment as a glaze to deepen the shadows. He made the lake glaze using a varnish based on tree resin (tree gum). The tree resin was possibly dissolved in spirit of turpentine or a similar solvent. He says the red lake glaze makes the shadows bluer (darker?). You could use Alizarin Crimson as a substitute for Red Lake.

Tests by scientists showed that a cross section of the Virgin of the Rocks was found to contain:

- The gesso ground.
- 1st drawing layer, directly on the gesso. It contains some large black particles.
- 1st imprimatura of lead white and some black.
- 2nd drawing layer containing fine black particles in a brown matrix
- 2nd imprimatura layer (containing less black and some lead-tin yellow
- Grey underpaint layer.
- Upper yellow paint (mainly lead-tin yellow).

Paintings in various stages, by Leonardo da Vinci:

Underdrawing (*Adoration of the Magi*).

Underpainting and Drawing (*St Jerome*).

Building up flesh tones (dead layers), (*Portrait of a Musician*)

Flesh tones before application of colour glaze (*The Virgin of the Rocks, London*)

Painting finished with colours and glazes, (*The Virgin of the Rocks, Louvre*)

Conclusion

Renaissance art combines the best of realism with the idea or concept in the mind of the painter. The Renaissance painter is not a mere copyist, but infuses the image of nature with his own ideas and spirit. Through the process of composition and using drawing in the forms of sketches, studies and cartoons, the artist gains a greater understanding of the world around him and his position in the world as an intelligent observer.

You cannot paint something well that you do not understand in terms of form, shape and volume, and how the various parts of the subject fit together, move, and work. The essence to understanding is through the process of drawing detailed studies of the parts of the subject. Notice how things move, change and behave and how these actions indicate the mind of the living subject. The artist should be an observer, a recorder, and a creator.

Remember to keep a sketchbook for drawing and experimenting with compositions and making notes and detailed study drawings. Build a resource or library of detailed studies and life drawings. Make drawings of anything of interest or possible use.

Practice and develop your painting techniques, such as painting in grisaille, mixing colours, blending and glazing. Practice painting crisp lines and edges. Work from the large shapes first and then proceed to detail after. Experiment with the various techniques and see what works for you. Remember, you don't have to use a 'Renaissance technique' if you don't wish to. You could use Renaissance composition with direct painting, 'alla prima' style, also.

I hope that this book has been of benefit to the reader, as a summary of Renaissance composition and art technique gleaned from my own studies of the Renaissance artists, their theories and their works. I wish you all the best in your creative endeavours. Bon Voyage!

APPENDIX

Appendix 1 - Concerning Perspective

Perspective is the method of creating an illusion of three dimensional depth on a two dimensional drawing or painting.

The main ways of creating the illusion of depth in a painting include:

- Overlapping objects
- Atmospheric Perspective (or Colour and Contrast perspective)
- Perspective of Disappearance
- Vertical Perspective
- Perspective of Size (known as Linear perspective)

Overlapping objects

Simply overlapping one shape with another implies that one object lies in front of another and give an illusion of the 3rd dimension of depth.

Overlapping Objects

Atmospheric Perspective

The colour of an object affects how we interpret the implied distance of an object represented on a surface. In nature distant objects such as trees or mountains appear lighter and bluer due to the haze of the intervening particles such as water vapour in the atmosphere. Closer objects in nature have more saturated colours and show more of their true colour or hue.

- Pales and cool colours tend to recede.
- Saturated and warm colours tend to advance

Atmospheric Perspective
(three towers at varying distances)

Saturated vs Pale Colours

Warm vs Cool Colours

Part of atmospheric perspective is perspective caused by tonal contrast. High contrast between two objects implies a larger separation of the two objects. Lower contrast implies that the objects are nearer to each other.

Perspective through
Contrast

Perspective of Disappearance

This is related to atmospheric perspective and the resolution of the eye. As an object becomes more distant to the observer the size of the details reduce until they disappear and are no longer visible. Only the large shapes of the object or group of objects is visible. The smallest and lowest contrast details disappear first as the object becomes more distant.

Reduction in Detail

Vertical Perspective

Objects which are positioned higher on the picture plane appear more distant.

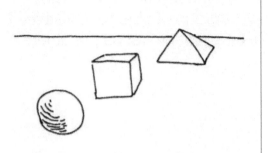

Perspective through
Vertical Position

Perspective of Size (known as Linear perspective)

The apparent size of objects reduce as they become more distant to us. The amount of reduction of size follows the mathematical laws of geometry and optics known as Linear Perspective.

Diminishing Size

Because objects get smaller as they get further away, a road with parallel sides will converge to a point on the horizon known as the 'vanishing point' (VP). Parallel lines converge toward the horizon if they are not parallel to the picture plane

Parallel Lines converge
toward the Horizon

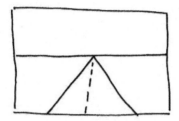

The Renaissance artists used a form of perspective known as one point or **single point perspective**. This system has one vanishing point (VP) located on the theoretical horizon of the viewer. When there are mountains or hills in the background the actual horizon may be higher than the theoretical horizon of the viewer (much as the tall buildings in the following diagram project above the horizon line). The horizontal lines of a building that go into the canvas will point toward the vanishing point.

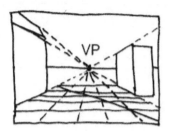

Single Point Perspective

After about the year 1500 AD a new perspective known as **two point perspective** was discovered.

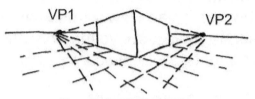

Two Point Perspective

Objects tilted toward the viewer appear shorter along their length, this is known as foreshortening. To find the centre of a foreshortened rectangle or square draw diagonals to find the foreshortened centre point.

Use diagonals to find
the centre, C, of a
forshortened Square
or Rectangle

A foreshortened circle becomes an ellipse. It is best to use a grid to plot your foreshortened circle. Use diagonals to find the centre of the foreshortened square containing the circle/ellipse. The centre of the foreshortened circle is at the centre of the foreshortened square surrounding it. The actual centre of the ellipse lies 'in front' of the foreshortened centre.

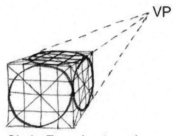

Circle Foreshortened

An arm foreshortened. The hand extending toward us is large and the arm tapers down to the distant shoulder. Note the implied overlapping lines at the joints of the wrist and elbow. This helps to establish which feature is in front of which.

Not Foreshortened

Foreshortened

To draw a figure foreshortened create a framework rectangle around your figure. Draw the foreshortened rectangle. Use diagonals to locate the centre of the foreshortened rectangle. Then find the centres of these two foreshortened half-rectangles using diagonals again. This gives the proportional framework for drawing the foreshortened figure. Draw the foreshortened figure using the framework as a guide.

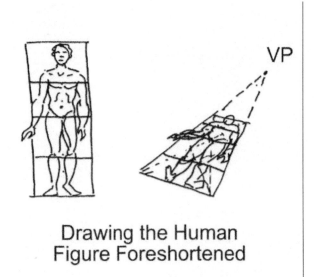

VP

Drawing the Human
Figure Foreshortened

Regularly spaced verticals

Use parallel diagonal lines to regularly space receding verticals or horizontals in perspective.

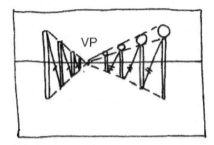

Use Parallel Diagonals
to regularly space
Verticals toward the
Vanishing Point

Drawing figures at various distances and locations.

From your Reference figure at A run a line back to the location of the required figure at X. Continue this line to the theoretical horizon to give the vanishing point. Draw a construction line from the head of the figure at A to the vanishing point, this will give the height of the figure at location, X.

Drawing figures in Proportion at any Location, X.

Constructing a Single Point Perspective Tiled Floor Grid

Draw a figure to the required size to act as your measurement stick (we will assume this figure is 6 feet in height). Draw a horizontal line at the base of the figure's feet. Establish your horizon line for however suites your composition.

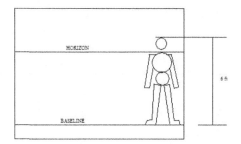

We will draw a tiled floor grid with 3 foot squares. Italian Renaissance artists may have used a grid based on the braccia, a measurement of about 2 feet. Establish your required vanishing point on the horizon line and drop a straight line down to the base of the canvas (this does not necessarily have to be vertical). Mark three foot divisions along the horizontal line at the base of the feet of the figure. Use your figure to establish the scale of the three foot divisions. Draw converging lines through each point to the vanishing point on the horizon.

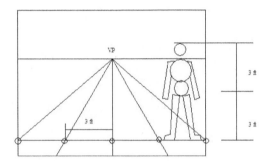

You can extend the 3 foot divisions off the canvas to draw more converging lines to the sides. Draw a horizontal line halfway between the baseline and the horizon. Measure two lengths of equal scale (here 12 feet has been selected). Notice that at the 50% line to the horizon, the 12 foot length is half the length as measured at the baseline. Draw a diagonal between these two lines of equal scale and mark where this diagonal crosses each converging line to the vanishing point.

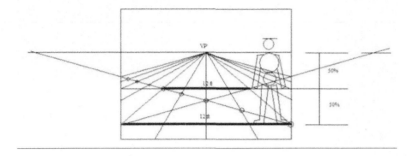

Draw horizontal lines between each point marked on the diagonal to establish your foreshortened floor grid.

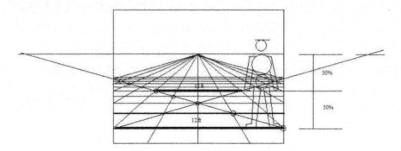

You can extend the grid further back toward the horizon by using more diagonals to step back into the distance toward the horizon and drawing the horizontals where the diagonal intersects with the lines that recede to the vanishing point.

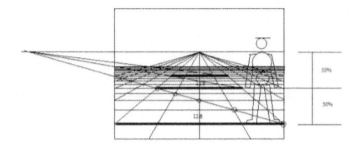

You can also establish a tiled wall grid using a similar method (establish the 50% (vertical) line based on the distance to the vanishing point or measure it from your horizontal grid 50% line and project vertically upwards).

Leonardo da Vinci, *Study for the Adoration of the Magi*

Appendix 2 - Silverpoint Drawing.

Silverpoint is a method of drawing with a silver stylus on a specially prepared ground. This was widely used during the Renaissance as graphite pencils had not yet been invented. The ground can be on a canvas or more usually a piece of paper. I use a piece of hard drawn 0.9mm sterling silver wire mounted in a 1mm mechanical pencil. The silver wire was obtained from a jewelry metal merchants.

I draw on a prepared Arches Smooth Watercolour paper (about 150gsm). Silverpoint needs a specially prepared paper surface that is slightly abrasive in order for the silver stylus to leave a mark. Silverpoint will not draw or make a mark on unprepared paper. I prepare the paper with an acrylic ground that I've formulated, which seems water resistant and produces a medium density of silverpoint shading. Colourfix Primer from Art Spectrum also works as a Silverpoint Ground.

Chris's Silverpoint Ground Recipe

In a jar mix:

- 2 teaspoons of Titanium White Acrylic paint (I used Reeves brand).
- 1 teaspoon of Titanium White pigment powder
- ½ a teaspoon of Zinc White artist's gouache
- A small amount (~1/8 teaspoon) of tube Watercolour to tint the ground (colour of choice)
- Add about 50ml of water and mix thoroughly to a thin creamy consistency.

(You should take all the normal safety precautions when handling and using art materials. Do not breathe in pigment powder, wear a suitable dust mask.)

Apply two coats of the ground to the paper of choice. Use a heavy water colour paper so it won't buckle or warp. Allow to dry between coats.

Following are some example silverpoint drawings that I have done. The first drawing, a Self-portrait, was sketched out in charcoal, then the outline gone over in Silverpoint. The charcoal was rubbed away and the shading done using fine hatching strokes.

The second drawing, a Unicorn, was again sketched loosely in charcoal and gone over in silverpoint, the charcoal was rubbed out leaving the silverpoint drawing, and then white pastel was used to colour the unicorn.

The third drawing sheet was done directly in Silverpoint, starting lightly and building up layers of hatching and shade to produce the final image. You cannot rub out silverpoint, so corrections are difficult if not impossible.

The silverpoint drawing will change slightly over time as the particles of silver tarnish with age.

By the author, Silverpoint sketches.

Self Portrait

Unicorn

Silverpoint Faces

Here are some examples of Renaissance silverpoint drawings:

Leonardo da Vinci, *Study of a horse and rider*

Leonardo da Vinci, *Study of a head*

Hans Holbein the Elder, *Ambrosius and Hans Holbein*

Albrecht Durer, *Self-portrait (Aged 13)*

Appendix 3 - Egg Tempera.

Egg Tempera is an Egg and Water emulsion medium used for painting during the Renaissance period. It has the ability to produce very fine line work and can be used for underpaintings under oil colour glazes. It dries rapidly compared to oil paints. It can also be painted into a layer of wet oil paint to give finely detailed finishing touches.

Traditional Egg Tempera

The following is the recipe for a traditional egg tempera medium.

- 1 part egg yolk (Separate the egg white from the yolk. Pierce the membrane of the yolk-sack and drain the whole of the yolk inside, into a container. Discard the egg white and yolk-sack membrane).
- 1 part distilled or boiled water (add to the egg yolk when cold). (Measure the water using a half egg shell as the measure).
- 10 drops or a small capful of white vinegar. (This acts as a preservative)

Mix well and emulsify the ingredients. It stores refrigerated for a month or so, depending on climate.

Egg-oil emulsion

Traditional egg tempera dries fast and doesn't allow for much mixing and blending of colour on the canvas. Traditional egg tempera also requires rigid supports such as a hardboard panel, as the paint layer becomes brittle as it dries. Use of an egg-oil emulsion (also known as *tempera grassa*) allows the paint to gain some of the characteristics of oil paint, whilst retaining the ability to use water as a thinner and paint fine details. The following egg-oil emulsion recipes were found on the internet.

Egg-oil emulsion - recipe 1

Add a small amount of linseed oil (about a capful thinned 50/50 with turpentine) to an egg yolk. Mixing thoroughly and then add an equal amount of water.

- 1 part Egg yolk,
- 1 part Linseed oil/thinner,
- 1 part Water,
- 1 capful White Vinegar.

Separate the yolk from the white and pierce the egg yolk membrane and drain the whole yolk into a small bowl. Mix the linseed oil (oil with thinner) a drop at a time vigorously into the yolk to obtain a good emulsion. Then add the water and mix. Store in a cool place. I would suggest not putting it into a fridge that contains food as the solvent vapours may poison the food.

Egg-oil emulsion - recipe 2

- 1 part Whole egg (yolk and white) (Strain through a fine sieve or cheesecloth).
- 1 part Oil mixed with turpentine (50/50).
- 1 part Water.
- 1 capful of white vinegar.

Store in a cool place. I would suggest not putting it into a fridge that contains food as the solvent vapours may poison the food.

Using Egg Tempera or Egg-Oil Emulsion

The medium is added to dry pigments, or alternatively, is mixed with gouache or tube watercolour paints. Gouache and watercolours contain organic compounds such as gum Arabic, glycerine and even honey, which could have an effect on the longevity of the medium but this is unknown for certain. Mix the amount of pigments (dry pigments, gouache or water colour) necessary for your session with the egg medium. The traditional egg tempera must be used on a gesso covered rigid support such as a wooden panel or hardboard. The egg-oil emulsion may be used over rigid or flexible supports with proper application of gesso. Apply multiple layers of thin tempera paint, use water as your solvent or thinner. Gradually reduce the amount of water used in each successive coat. The tempera or emulsion can also be used to paint wet in wet into a fresh layer of oil paint.

Tempera painting technique

The following are basic guidelines for painting in Egg Tempera. For more information consult a book on Egg Tempera painting. I recommend, 'Egg Tempera Painting' by Koo Schadler.

Temper your pigments correctly: Add the right amount of egg medium to your pigment powder or tube watercolours. The tempera paint should dry to a surface with a slight sheen to it. It shouldn't be glossy (too much egg medium), and it shouldn't be powdery (too little medium). You may dilute the tempered paint with water as required, the water will evaporate and make no difference to the tempera adhesion, but it will affect the transparency and intensity of the colour.

Work in many layers of thin paint: Build up your tempera painting in successive layers of thin paint. Apply a brushstroke of paint to the panel surface and move on to the next area, leaving it to dry to the touch before working over it. Do not overwork the paint as you may lift underlying layers of paint that are not cured. (Egg tempera dries to the touch rapidly in minutes but does not fully cure for 6 to 12 months).

Use a dry brush technique: Use a 'dry' brush technique with hatching or stippling to apply the paint. You want to avoid wet blobs or puddles of paint on the surface that will take a longer time to dry. Use a cloth to blot excess paint from your brush.

Support and Ground

Traditional egg tempera requires a rigid support such as a wood panel or Masonite (hardboard) as it becomes brittle as it dries. Traditionally a Rabbit skin glue size and traditional gesso (rabbit skin glue and chalk or hydrated plaster) is used to prime the panel prior to painting. I have experimented with an acrylic primer (Art Spectrum Colourfix Primer (White)) and have found that to work well, providing a good surface and adhesion. However the Colourfix primer has a rough tooth caused by the presence of silica particles, which produces a sandpaper like texture, and I expect it to wear the brush bristles down quite rapidly. You should use soft-bristled brushes (synthetics or sables) for painting with egg tempera. When sanding or abrading, (especially silica-based products, like Colourfix primer), wear suitable protective dust masks and protective clothing.

Botticelli, *The Birth of Venus (tempera grassa on canvas)*.

Appendix 4 - What did Leonardo da Vinci look like?

Whilst looking at the painting, *Portrait of Fra Luca Pacioli*, which contains an unknown figure on the right of the painting, I noticed a resemblance between the unknown figure and paintings of a young man that were in the catalogue for the exhibition 'Leonardo: Painter in the Court of Milan'. These portraits had all been done by associates or students of Leonardo, as well as the *'Portrait of a Musician'* attributed to Leonardo himself.

In the *Portrait of Luca Pacioli*, there are strong similarities to the composition of *The Last Supper* by Leonardo. The central figure of Luca Pacioli is similar in some ways to the central figure of Christ in the Last Supper. He is placed in a central triangular composition and is behind a table, much like in the Last Supper. Pacioli's hands are spread somewhat like Christ's hands. Leonardo was a student of Fra Luca Pacioli and the geometric solids in this painting are based on those drawn by Leonardo to illustrate Pacioli's book *'De Divina Proportione'*, (The Divine Proportion). The painting also uses a black background similar to that used by many of Leonardo's portraits whilst in Milan.

Portrait of Luca Pacioli

The *Portrait of Luca Pacioli* has been attributed to Jacopo de Barbari based on the evidence of a lettered cartouche within the painting (located near Pacioli's left hand and directly below the unknown figure). The painting has been dated as being produced around 1495 to 1500.

The cartouche contains the inscription IACO.BAR. VIGENNIS. P. 1495, and has an annoying fly close to obscuring the last digit of the date (1495). The attribution of the painting to Jacopo de Barbari has been questioned due to the painting's different style and composition. I have compared the portrait with other paintings by Jacopo de Barbari (using internet images) and its finish and realism seems a whole step or class above Jacopo's usual painting technique.

I believe the cartouche inscription could be a message by Leonardo da Vinci. The cartouche can be read as: JAC[OPO] BAR[BARI]

VIGENNIS P[IXIT] 1495 (with the annoying fly almost obscuring the last digit of the date). The literal interpretation of the cartouche would therefore be: Jacopo Barbari, aged 20, painted in 1495, with the fly being symbolic of annoyance. This interpretation is probably invalid, as Jacopo was born sometime between 1450 to 1470, and would have been about 30 years of age in the year 1495. The key to the cartouche lies in the interpretation of VIGENNIS.

THE CLUE: VIGENNIS

IN LATIN: Equals VICENIS (Which means, 20, and is disguised as the erroneous age of the painter. Leonardo, Luca Pacioli and possibly Jacopo Barbari were all over 30 years of age at this date).

AS AN ANAGRAM: VICENIS can be rearranged as the Italian phrase, VINCI SE ("Vinci himself").

The cartouche could be a hidden clue and joke of Leonardo Da Vinci as the painter or co-painter of the portrait and as the unknown man standing behind the left shoulder of Luca Pacioli. Leonardo is also possibly referring to himself or his cipher with the presence of the 'annoying fly'.

The portrait of the young man to the right is very similar in appearance to the figure in Leonardo's *Portrait of a Musician*, and is also similar to a red or ginger haired man depicted in several portraits by associates or students of Leonardo.

It would make sense if the unknown figure in this painting is Leonardo da Vinci, Luca Pacioli's famous student and illustrator of his work, '*De Divina Proportione*'. The unknown figure certainly looks like a self-portrait by an artist with his eyes staring directly out at the viewer.

Illustration of a geometric solid, by Leonardo da Vinci, from *De Divina Proportione*.

The geometric solid, a rhombicuboctahedron, appears in the *Portrait of Luca Pacioli* in the upper left.

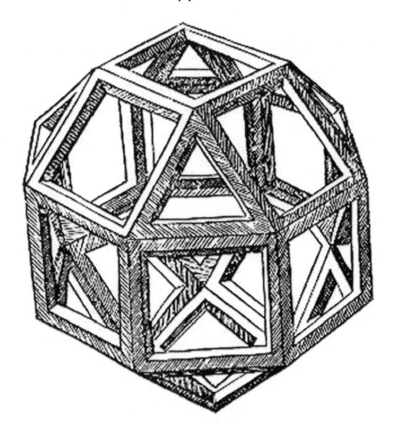

Facsimile of the cartouche inscription, a hidden message and joke by Leonardo?

Leonardo's Portrait of a Musician

The *Portrait of a Musician* is a painting attributed to Leonardo da Vinci. It is dated to about 1490 when Leonardo was working for Ludovico Sforza at the Court of Milan.

The sitter of the portrait is unknown. Several suggestions have been offered to his identity including: Franchino Gaffurio, a musician from the Cathedral of Milan; a monk, Leonardo Pistoia, from the Court of Cosimo de Medici; or an anonymous member of the Court of Milan.

The person in the unfinished portrait is holding a piece of parchment upon which is written a musical score. The sitter has a cap, curly reddish hair, a strong chin with dimple, a straight nose, heavy lidded eyes, full lips and strong cheek bones. These features are identical to the unknown man in the *Portrait of Luca Pacioli*.

Siegfried Woldhek, an illustrator from the Netherlands, has claimed that the *'Portrait of a Musician'* is one of three self-portraits by Leonardo, the others being: *The Red Chalk Portrait* (Turin); and the figure of *Vitruvian Man*.

Leonardo was noted by the writer, Vasari, as a fine musician who played the lyre, and who was possibly also a composer of music.

Portrait of an Unknown Young Man by Ambrogio de Predis

This *Portrait of a Young Man* is very similar in appearance to the figure in Leonardo's *Portrait of a Musician*. We can see the same strong chin with dimple, wavy reddish hair of a similar cut, heavy lidded eyes, full lips, strong cheek bones, the nose has a slight crookedness but is reasonably straight. The figure is dressed with a cap and fur collared robe.

Ambrogio de Predis is recorded as a collaborator with Leonardo on the painting, *The Virgin of the Rocks*, which was painted whilst Leonardo was in Milan. Ambrogio also worked at the Court of Milan, as a portrait painter.

This portrait appears to be the same unknown man depicted in the *Portrait of Luca Pacioli* and Leonardo's *Portrait of a Musician*. The artist was a close associate of Leonardo da Vinci.

The Archinto Portrait.

This portrait is presumed to represent Francesco di Bartolomeo Archinto. The identification of the sitter is traditional.

A small parchment scroll held by the sitter has a cryptic monogram which has at one time been thought to be composed of the letters, AMPRF, which was taken to mean, Ambrogio Predis Fecit (Ambrogio de Predis made this). It is now thought that the painting is the work of Marco Oggiono, a student of Leonardo whilst in Milan, based on stylistic considerations.

The scroll also records that the painter is 20 years old. The monogram could be read equally well as MAR ANO 20 (Mar[co] aged 20). Leonardo was born about 1452 and would have been aged 42 in 1494 when this portrait was painted. Marco Oggiono was born about 1475 and would have been about 20 which is in line with this interpretation of the inscription. Another possible alternative is that the, 20, refers to the Latin term 'Vicenis' which is an anagram of 'Vinci se' ('Vinci himself'), and could therefore be a cryptic reference to the identity of the sitter, Leonardo.

Again, this portrait appears similar to the figure depicted by Ambrogio de Predis in Portrait of a Young Man, sharing all the same features, including the style of dress.

Lucan portrait of Leonardo da Vinci

The *Lucan portrait of Leonardo da Vinci* dates from the end of the 15th century and has been claimed as a self-portrait of Leonardo. This claim is based on a comparison of the portrait with several other portraits of Leonardo, including: *The Portrait in Red Chalk* (Turin), and a *Portrait of Leonardo* by Francesco Melzi.

The portrait is painted on a wooden panel upon the back of which is an inked inscription reading PINXIT MEA in mirror writing. This portrait conforms to the others considered so far in the wavy reddish hair, heavy lidded eyes, full lips, straight nose, and strong cheek bones.

The inscription PINXIT-MEA.

Portrait of a man in red chalk (Leonardo)

The *Portrait of a man in red chalk* (Turin), is generally accepted as a self-portrait of Leonardo in his old age. The pose, a three-quarter view facing to the viewer's right, is similar to that in Leonardo's *Portrait of a Musician*. The likeness is similar to that of the figure based on Leonardo in Raphael's, *School of Athens*.

Portrait of Leonardo by his pupil and assistant, Francesco Melzi

Andrea Verrocchio's **Statue of David**, said to be a portrait of the young Leonardo.

Figure of a youth from Leonardo's '*Adoration of the Magi'* which is said to be a portrait of Leonardo. There is a strong resemblance in the pose of this figure to Verrocchio's statue of David.

Comparison of the Portraits

Here we see the portraits of what appears to be the same person, allowing for stylistic variations of the various artists. We can note the following characteristics in all of these portraits: a strong chin with dimple, long reddish hair with wavy curls and a similar cut, heavy lidded eyes, full lips, strong cheek bones, and a similar costume in all paintings. It appears that these may all be portraits of the same person. All these paintings are attributed to known associates of Leonardo da Vinci and it seems quite possible that these are all portraits of the young Leonardo.

We can compare the *Statue of David* by Verrocchio, said by Vasari to be a portrait of the young Leonardo, with the *Portrait of a Musician* by Leonardo. The features of both are compatible allowing for stylistic variation. We can also compare the two paintings and drawing. The poses are all ¾ view facing to the right and the main features are similar, eyes, nose, lips and cheek bones. The Lucan portrait (lower left) differs in that the sitter is looking toward the viewer rather than off to the right. The red chalk portrait seems to deviate a bit in the portrayal of the nose, but this could be an effect of the age of the sitter. It seems likely that these are all portraits of Leonardo da Vinci at various times throughout his life. This is not a definite certainty, as I have not viewed the original paintings, and my hypothesis is based on a qualitative assessment, not on scientific study of the paintings. Perhaps those with the appropriate resources might like to investigate this more scientifically. At the moment I consider this conclusion regarding the portraits as a reasonable assumption based on the evidence seen in the images of the paintings. I also would like to note that I am not the first to suggest the similarity of many of these portraits, and that Siegfried Woldhek, a Dutch illustrator, has previously claimed that 'The Portrait of a Musician' is one of three self-portraits by Leonardo.

One thing to note, when comparing the various portraits of Leonardo, is that the concept of a 'photographic likeness' was unknown in the Renaissance and that a true likeness was probably not considered as important as we would consider it nowadays. In the Renaissance the portrait was to improve on nature using the ideal platonic conception in the mind of the artist. We should not expect Renaissance portraits of the same person, portrayed by different artists, to be 'identical' in a modern photographic sense.

Glossary

Chiascuro – 'light and dark'. Chiasuro is the Italian term for modelling the form in a painting by using light and dark tones. High chiascuro with strong light and dark tones was used by Leonardo da Vinci and later adopted by Baroque artists such as Carravagio.

Dead Colouring (Dead Layer) – Dead colour (or dead layer) is a layer of paint made with pale versions of the final colour intended for the painting. This dead layer (of pale colours) is normally glazed over to achieve the final required colour and tonal intensity.

Decoro – 'decorum'. Decorum is considered as 'appropriateness'. The pose, clothes, and character of the subjects in a painting should consistently act in a manner to show the mind and character of the subject. Decorum is also considered the appropriateness of a painted subject to its surroundings, such as in a church or a domestic dwelling.

Designo – design, drawing, draughtsmanship and composition.

Glaze – A transparent layer of coloured paint made by thinning the transparent or translucent paint pigment down with a quantity of medium. (Compare with 'scumble').

Golden Mean (Golden Ratio) – A proportional ratio with peculiar properties, the ratio of the two parts being equal to the ratio of one part to the whole. Numerically being approximately equivalent to 1:0.618.

Grazia – 'grace'. In Renaissance art theory paintings should be endowed with 'grace'. Grace is a 'softness', 'charm', and 'gentleness', with no harsh transitions.

Grisaille – A tonal underpainting mainly in grey or greyish monochrome. Commonly used in the Venetian technique. The grisaille was usually finished with a coloured final layer of transparent glazes and opaque scumbles of paint.

Harmonic Grid – A method of dividing the canvas with orthogonal and diagonal lines based on certain proportions such as the musical proportions (q.v.) or the golden mean (q.v.). The harmonic grid is used to aid in the positioning and alignment of key features in the composition of the painting.

Intonaco – a translucent layer of paint, coloured or toned, and applied all over the canvas during the underdrawing stage.

Imprimtura – See 'intonaco'

Leonardo technique – A recreated oil painting technique based upon the methods of Leonardo da Vinci. Using a verdaccio (q.v.) underdrawing, dead colours (q.v.), and glazing of colours (see 'glaze').

Maniera – 'manner'. The 'style' of an artist or school of painters.

Musical proportions – The musical proportions are proportions based on certain ratios which are made of small whole numbers. These musical proportions which underlie musical harmony were applied to architecture by the Ancient Greeks and were recorded by the Roman writer, the architect Vitruvius. Later, in medieval and Renaissance times, these musical ratios were applied to the composition of paintings. The most important musical ratios are considered to be the harmonious ratios corresponding to: the octave (1:2), the perfect fifth (2:3), and the perfect fourth (3:4).

Natura - 'nature'. The theory of basing painting and drawing on the imitation of nature as a starting point and reference. However, in accordance with neo-platonic philosophy 'nature' must be improved upon in accordance with the platonic ideal in the mind of the painter.

Negative space – The space between objects on the canvas. (Compare with Positive Space).

Northern technique – Also known as Flemish technique. A method of oil painting in many layers developed in Northern Europe and perfected by the Van Eyck brothers in Flanders. This early oil painting technique achieved a high degree of realism and luminous colour.

Order – Different self-contained styles, such as the Doric, Ionic and Corinthian orders of architecture.

Perspective – The science of portraying the illusion of three dimensions of form and space through the use of techniques such as diminishing size and variation of contrast and colour.

Positive space – The space on the canvas occupied by an object. (Compare with Negative Space).

Proportion – The ratio of different sizes of objects or the spaces between them. The method of measuring and positioning objects.

Rule of thirds – A method of dividing the canvas in three (usually equal) parts vertically and horizontally and using these divisions to position objects within the painting composition.

Scumble – A translucent layer of paint made by thinning down opaque pigment with medium and applying thinly to the surface of the painting. (Compare with 'glaze').

Sfumato - 'smokiness'. A painting technique with softly blended tones and no hard lines, perfected by Leonardo da Vinci. The prime example being the Mona Lisa.

Silverpoint – A method of drawing with a silver metal stylus on a prepared surface or ground. Commonly used in the Renaissance, before the development of graphite pencils.

Tempera – A medium of painting usually using egg as the primary binder for the pigment. Egg tempera can use water as a thinner and therefore it can be used for painting fine details such as thin lines. Sometimes used for underdrawings in oil painting techniques.

Tempera Grassa – A form of tempera painting using an egg-oil medium that gains some of the desirable qualities of oil paint, such as flexibility of the dry paint film and a slower drying time.

Venetian technique – The technique of oil painting developed in Renaissance Venice. Usually using a canvas support with an underdrawing, a grisaille (q.v.) layer, and glazing of colours (see 'glaze').

Verdaccio – A thin paint layer of dark greenish or brownish paint used in a tonal underdrawing or underpainting.

Printed in Great Britain
by Amazon

41480590R00110